Sandy
Brown

Sandy Brown

I think it's freedom.
I am hooked on the exhilaration of freedom.
Freedom to do anything I want.

Sandy
Brown

Published 2003 by Marston House
Marston Magna, Yeovil BA22 8DH
in association with

British Library Cataloguing-in-Publication Data
A catalogue record for this book is
available from the British Library

Photographs by John Russell, John Andow,
Takeshi Yasuda, Russell Baader

Front cover photograph: Softly thrown dish, 28 cm wide
Back cover: Two figures, 40 and 30 cm high
Title page: Parthenogenesis, painting 183 x 168 cm
This page: Goddess, 55 cm high

Printed by Remous Ltd, Milborne Port, Sherborne, Dorset

Introduction

The work of artists and makers conveys messages about the individual. Their creativity, materials, techniques and issues of concern. Through a sequence of events, we perceive the form, colour, surface and texture of an object. The question of how we feel about it may ultimately depend upon our actually being able to touch, to gauge the substance, and hear its resonance. When the total experience is consistently pleasing, the result can be magical.

Those who know Sandy Brown's work will be familiar with the economy and cogency of her distinctive language. Inventive, deliberate shapes, a gentle palette of metallic oxides used spontaneously in response to each form with textures ranging from the buttery to the earthy. The work invites handling. Its substance confirms our impression of a sensuous and poetic energy.

Each phase of Sandy's life has honed her talents and nature. Whilst working at the Daisei pottery in Japan high levels of skill were established. These have evolved so that Sandy can now pursue her goal of 'letting go'. Whether making pots for use or contemplation, they clearly express her secure roots and yet her freedom to fly with the gods.

One year, having commissioned an outsize pair of candlesticks as my wife's Christmas surprise, we sef off on a mystery journey which ended at Sandy's studio. It took a nanosecond for Jennie to realise that the two magnificent structures which greeted us were the reason for our visit. Their scale, sense of fun, the buxom figures dancing between the candles and the colours were perfect for our carpeted dining table. The experience was then enriched by lunch with Sandy on her ceramics. Food has never looked better. Born to an organic farming family, Sandy lives by a set of values that permeate her work and give it a wonderful integrity.

John Makepeace

It feels like flying

I feel as free as a child playing, happy, joyful, delighted that what to me feels like just doodling can be so wonderful.

I think my training as an artist helps me to make things happen when I want them to. To be in a state when I have not a care in the world, when whatever happens will be okay. It does not guarantee that it will be okay, but it is essential that I believe, in the moment of creativity, that whatever happens will be okay. That way I can take risks, I can be free, knowing that it will be fine. I am in a state of acceptance during creativity. Later, I judge what I have done. And judgement is a gut response: 'Yes, it's flowing,' or 'Oh dear, no.' And that is really all there is to it. It means I am living in the moment *now*.

When I accept invitations to demonstrate at art colleges or potters' or artists' groups I often do a 'spontaneity demonstration', because I do not want just to show something I have done before. I want to show and talk about the essence of creativity, to show what it is. Some writers have said about my work that it is a 'performance', and that always puzzled me, as I mostly work alone and have never thought about what I do as a performance. But I think it would be the same if it were a performance.

It is improvising, as a jazz musician improvises. Keith Jarrett, my favourite piano player and a wonderful jazz improviser, says that he does not practise, he just performs. He starts with one note and it leads into the next. That is what I do in clay and in colour.

'Improvised Plate with Three Scrunches'
25 cm wide

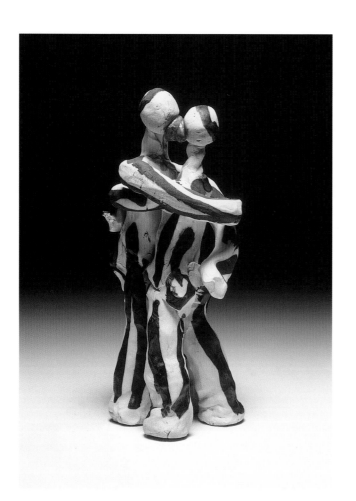

Discovery and rediscovery

I have been making figures now for twenty years or so. They started initially as a therapy, for me to work out my own feelings and my history. The first ones were raw with pain and desire to escape into fantasies. Now the reason to make a figure is to find out what the next one will be. It is a journey of discovery. I observe how visitors to the studio respond to these figures. What is personal to me is also reflected in the wider culture; in feminism, the growing sense that to be female is to be celebrated and that contemporary female icons in art can now be accepted. I see that my latest figures, female, have a sense of their inner strength, their calmness and power.

Left: 'Lovers', 30 cm high

Opposite: Millennium women, 2 m high. 'Ulana' (left), 'Kara (right)

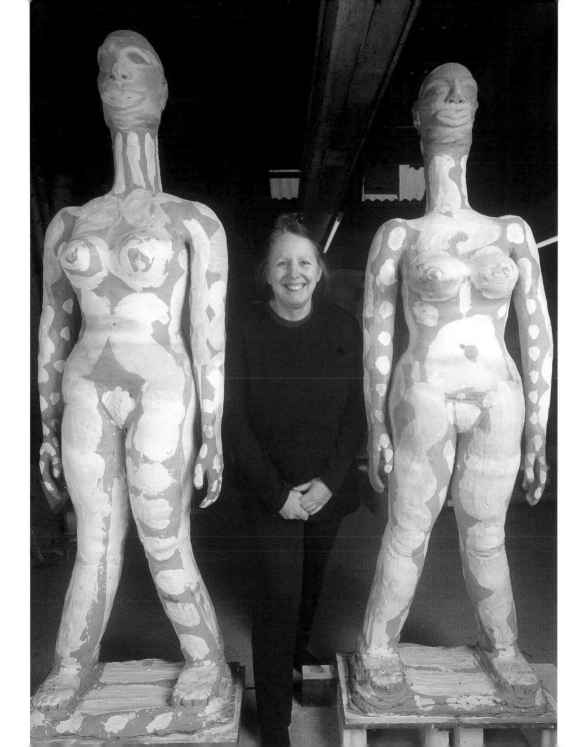

Textured slab platter with handles,
48 cm wide

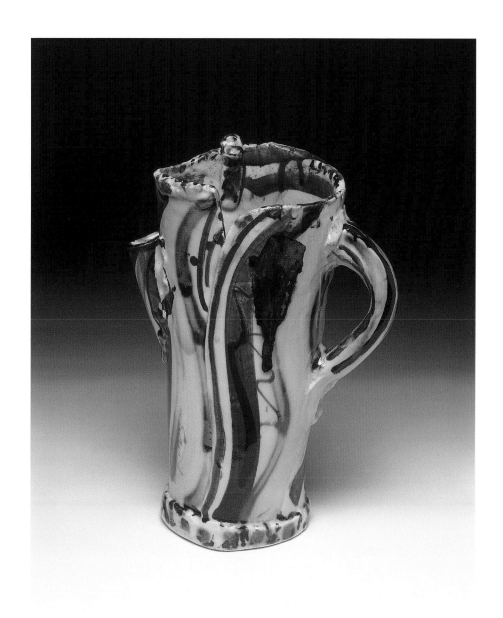

Rolled slab pitcher,
40 cm high

Is it good?

I assess my work after the firing and observe my gut response. Do I like this one or not? If I do, it's in the show. Sometimes I try to analyse why a particular piece works. Analysis of the form is very useful in deepening my understanding of what works and it helps me to develop new forms, but analysis does not seem to work with the painting. Actually that is not entirely true; analysis does work a little, but only so far. If I say, for example, that the painting on that piece has worked because of the wide swish of cobalt blue with the little doodle of more cobalt over it, with a few blobs of peach glaze beside it, then I think that will work if I do it again. But it doesn't. If I do it again on another form, then it is not the same. It looks hesitant, self-conscious, out of balance. and the conclusion I have come to is that the reason it does not work the second time is that I am not in the same free state that I was before. I am trying. What make the first one work is not the arrangement of cobalt and peach and the width of the swish, but the state I was in when I did it. The arrangement of the cobalt swish is the evidence of my state of mind, or state of freedom. If I don't like it then I have to ask myself why, and to check whether my response is valid or not. I can often dismiss pieces too early, when I am, for example, disappointed that some vision I might have had has not materialised, or that the colour balance has not worked. If the colour balance is wrong then I am usually right to dismiss it. The natural flow, or my instinct, has a structure and balance of its own, and if I give it its head it will create a painting on the pot which is much richer than I could have done if I had thought about it or prepared it in advance. My work has developed over the years, without much interference from me. By observing my responses to new work carefully, I programme my intuition for the future.

Softly thrown pot with scrunch,
50 cm high

Above: Textured slab platter, 42 cm wide

Opposite: Raised slab platter with handles, 50 cm wide

Loosening up

The painting of the pots started when I could not resist the urge to scribble in the soft white slip. I apply the thick creamy slip when the pot is hard enough to absorb the water without collapsing - leather hard - and after a few minutes the slip is ready to doodle on. You cannot do it again if it doesn't work, so it is a great way of loosening up. If I think, for example, 'This is a great plate, the shape is good, it has worked well on the wheel in its softness and generosity,' and I become afraid of messing it up because it is a good plate, then I am lost. I might as well drop it on the floor. The only way to work is not to worry about failing, not to worry that it will not be good. In other words, to allow oneself the freedom to fail. So that is what I do. If I sense that I am becoming tense, I say, 'It's only a plate, plenty more where that came from,' and then I can feel my body relax, let go, and something happens: I can make lines in the soft slip as easily as doodling. After I had discovered how easy it is to make marks in the slip, I extended that spirit into the way I use brushes and trailers to apply the colours.

Plates, approx 30 cm wide. All slab made except for top row centre and middle row left which are softly thrown, and bottom row left which is improvised.

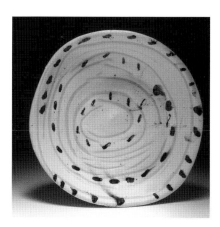

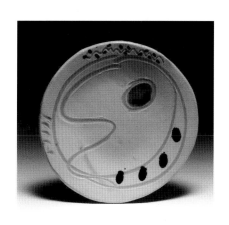

Softly thrown dish, 58 cm wide

Slab painting, 30 cm wide

Left: Softly thrown dish, 55 cm diameter

Pots in everyday life

I had an upbringing lacking in the arts, and did not
discover ceramics and art until I arrived in Japan when
I was 22. However, I do now realise the importance
during my childhood of seeing my mother always
making, making, making things as I grew up. I think
it is natural to make things.

And so now I live with pots, use pots, make pots
for other people to use. Using pots enhances our
creativity and inspires us to think more imaginatively
about food and its presentation. I feel quite deprived
when going out for a meal to find nothing but those
ubiquitous white plates. It is as if theatre were always
acted on a blank stage. An opportunity lost. The
experience of dining can be so much richer if we use
contemporary ceramics. That is a large part of what
motivates me to make pots for use.

Pedestal dish, 40 cm wide

Below: 'Cheeky Pot', 43 cm wide

Rediscovering lost childhood

When working at the wheel I deliberately allow it to turn slowly, so that the clay is almost out of control. That way the pot will become off-centre, and have the sensuality of my hand movements on it. I like it when there are occasionally lumps of unkneaded clay in the mix which cause the pot to be softly warped. I like it when the pot has some movement in the finished form. A lot of people think my thrown pots are not made on the wheel as they are so irregular, and they ask me how I did it: 'Was it coiled?' 'Handbuilt?' I consider that a compliment.

I keep my forms relatively simple. Many of them are based on what I saw as a child in my grandmother's dairy. I loved my grandmother: she was a buxom farmer's wife, always cooking, and in the farmhouse there was a dairy next to the kitchen. There were interesting pots and dishes in there; it was full of interesting things. That is where my cheese dish form (cloche) comes from, as I used to love going into the dairy and lifting up the lid to see what was underneath. Sometimes it was a summer pudding, or a moulded bread-and-butter pudding, or cheese, or some cooked roast beef, or a freshly-made cake. I have hardly changed the form I make from the one my grandmother had, just added some feet to the platter and simplified the handle of the dome. I like the simplicity and sculptural strength of the form.

I also remember seeing large dishes, which I now know were cream pans - huge open bowls, generous and open-hearted. Now I like to make simple bowl shapes, and allow them to warp slightly while soft on the wheel, so that they are breathing and alive.

In the dairy were milk jugs, with a crocheted cloth on the top to keep the flies off, and lidded pots with pickles and chutneys in them. Although I believed that my inspiration all started in Japan, I now know that I was also affected as a child by my grandmother's dairy, her kitchen, and her meals. Everything starts in childhood, and it takes time to rediscover it.

'Cloche', 35 cm wide

Lasagne dish
35 cm wide

Teapot, 30 cm high

Teapot, 32 cm high

Living with pots

For part of the work I make I choose to have a framework around the spontaneity: making pots for everyday use.

I started work in Japan over thirty years ago, where I lived for five years, and that is where I came to love experiencing art in daily life, and creating ritual in the every day. I found in Japan people not afraid to use pots of high value in the way, say, that some people in the West are not afraid to wear designer shoes after paying out several hundred pounds per pair.

What I saw in Japan was that a potter's art is valued above all others, and that potters get to be Human National Treasures, whereas painters and sculptors do not. Chefs and cooks use pots made by top studio potters in the best restaurants. Top chefs in Japan are experts on contemporary ceramics, use them, and are inspired by them. And potters work as artists do - they make individual pieces with as much consideration and individuality as painters and sculptors in the West.

Softly thrown pot with lid, 40 cm high

'Elephant Girl', 25 cm high

'Delicious platter', 40 cm wide

Sharing and doing

I want my work to be immediate, to express the moment in which it was made. I do not want it to express hours and hours and days of laborious planning. I want it to look fresh, as if it has just been done. I want the actual moment of impulsive creativity to be there, so that you can see it and respond to it at a gut level. I want you to feel what I felt when I did it: fun, exhilaration and freedom. I want to show you the excitement of the now, of the raw energy of abandon.

That is why I nearly always keep the natural white slip colour as the background, so that you can see the marks made by the brush as the glazes go on, and the squirts of colour from the slip trailer. A slip trailer is not for the faint-hearted. It needs courage, like diving into the deep end, and you do not have a second chance.

So, with about seven or eight colours, using strong oxides such as cobalt, manganese and copper, alongside some commercial stains applied with wide brushes, thin brushes and slip trailers, I have built up a vocabulary of mark-making as if I were an abstract painter. Potters often talk about 'decorating' pots. I am not decorating my pots. I look at Patrick Heron's work, or Roger Hilton's or Bert Irvin's, and I know I am doing the same thing. To call this 'decorating' belittles it. It is part of the serious language of painting.

'Dance of clay and glazes',
textured platter, 60 cm wide

'Out of the Downward Spiral',
clay painting, 50 cm wide

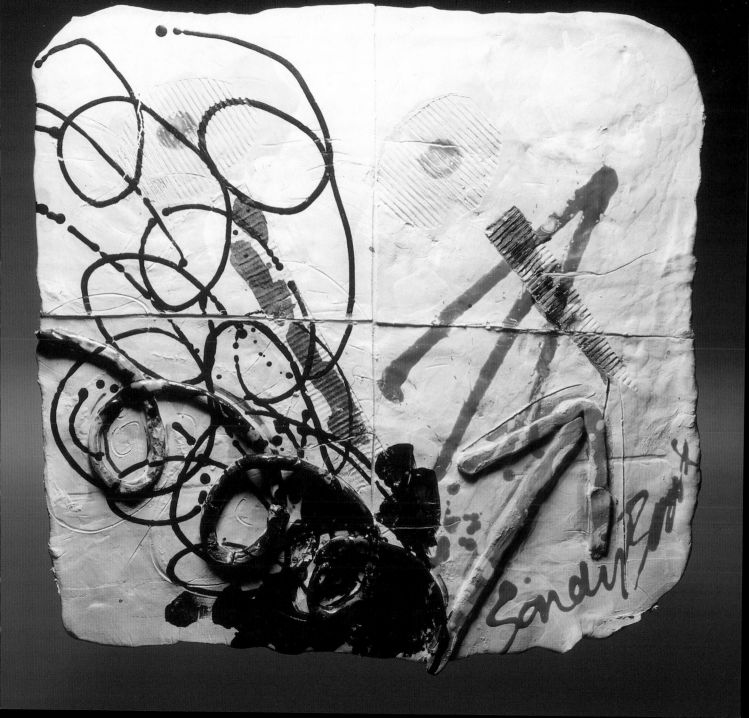

'Spiral figure', 15 cm high

Spirals in time

I take another route into sculptural forms, which are currently abstract but organic in structure, alive, almost breathing. When I teach students to loosen up I often give them a project to help them to do so, which is to make thirty things in thirty minutes. I set the clock, and they go to work until the bell rings. Often I do it too, and it is quite amazing what happens. It sounds as though this is a joke: light, easy, playful, and in one sense it is, but it also can be quite profound. Things can appear from the subconscious, forgotten things, feelings we did not know we had, symbols we did not know were important. I use this to gain 'seedcorn': ideas for new projects, and some of them I choose to develop. Over the years the sculptures arising from this way of working have expressed fertility, fecundity, fear, sexuality, tranquillity, loss and abundance.

As I write, I seem to be obsessed with spirals. They seem to be a metaphor for life. Our lives are like spirals; we grow, we sometimes think we are back at the same place we were years and years ago, but in fact we are further along the spiral. I certainly feel that in my latest simple thrown dishes I have progressed in a spiral. After a few years spent making life-sized female figures, tall standing organic forms, standing clay canvasses, I now find myself almost back at the beginning, making softly thrown dishes. When I pick each one up, immediately after throwing, in its creamy vulnerable softness, I let it move in my hands, and it changes shape.

Life being like a spiral shows in my latest abstract pieces, which themselves are composed of soft clay spirals, stacked up, figurative and in families. Some other recent abstract sculptural pieces are hard to explain. Perhaps they are about independence, energy, or fertility, or inner peace, possibly all of these things. And perhaps they will communicate something personal to others. I think that is one of the strengths of art: what is the most personal is also universal. It allows me to do things for myself, and others to make their own connections. Certainly the pieces in this series look natural in the same way that a tree does, or a coral reef, and relate back to earlier fertility pieces which included lots of balls which are either eggs or peas or seeds. The balls are now getting bigger, less egg-like, but still hinting at evolution, development and infinite growth. Such pieces need time to gestate and I give them this by having several on the go at once. Moving around from one series to another allows me to return fresh to develop them. I am happiest when I am doing something I have never done before; that intensity of new experience, like arriving in a new country.

Right: 'Organo-phosphorus', 40 cm high

Below: 'Totem', 25 cm high

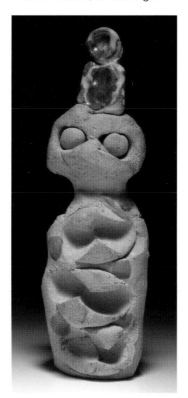

'Horse', 22 cm high

Inspiration

I have often wondered where my painting comes from. I know that art students are required to recognize their influences, but I have not been fully aware of this. Sometimes I try to please people by saying, 'Picasso' or 'Jackson Pollock', but the truth is that my style was developed before I even knew the work of these artists.

I can say that Japan was the biggest influence, in ways that I am still discovering. For example, I saw some wonderful free expressionist painting on ceramics with slip, literally a throwing of the slip from the ladle through the air and its being 'caught' on a big dish; I saw some robust handling of the clay which was dangerous in its fearlessness; I saw some delightful sensuous throwing of porcelain, which in the West is known for its translucency and fine brittleness, whereas in fact it can be fat and deliciously, erotically juicy.

I saw some paintings in Japan done by monks, after their meditation, in which a spontaneous burst of energy was captured in a single movement. I think that is closest in spirit to my work.

I like it in my work when, for example, a large mass of one colour is balanced by a few squiggles; a big space of a certain shape punctuated with a splash of cobalt; a few lines of copper oxide green may need a wavy peach-glaze brush mark beside them; a big bold trailing of dark manganese oxide can be balanced by a large splodge of pink, or a few copper green dots, and so on and so on.

Serving platter, 42 cm wide

'Estuary'. 52 cm wide

Candelabrum with dancers,
54 cm high

Letting go

It is about letting go, and not being in control. When it is working best I am observing what is happening, rather than leading. I am not consciously doing something; it is an instinctive impulse, and then I have to follow, with no choice in the matter.

Sometimes people have a fear of letting go, and occasionally that means that there are strong feelings or impulses being repressed: what will happen when they are released? To let go, to be spontaneous, is actually a very serious thing, as one has to deal with the consequences. I have learned a great deal about myself this way; I have faced my demons. I think that one reason why being spontaneous is so important to me in my work is that I was not able to do this as a child. Now I can. And when I see what comes, the structure of my clay work and my painting, particularly in the abstract forms and painting, there is no anarchy or chaos. Instinct has a structure and order of its own, and it seems to be the very structure of nature; look around you, there is an order and structure which is organic, irregular and assymetrical.

Sculpture and painting on sculpture

I love to make sculptural forms and figures. These have arisen out of doodling with the clay.

Some sculptural forms are essentially standing clay canvases, in which all the thumbprints and fingermarks and pushing and squidging show up in the clay itself, and the rough edges are allowed to stay rough, as happens in the Earth. I make slabs by spreading the clay on cloth with the heel of my hand, which gives a beautiful undulating rhythm to the surface. Then I build up several slabs to give height to the form, and where the slabs join there will inevitably be cracks, which I repair by adding obvious clay 'plasters'. Clay can look so wonderfully geological when it is treated robustly.

Later, painting with colourful textured glazes complements the forms. The sculptures have a back and a front, with different painting on each side. These are monumental pieces. They allow me to integrate form and painting, with a similar spirit in both.

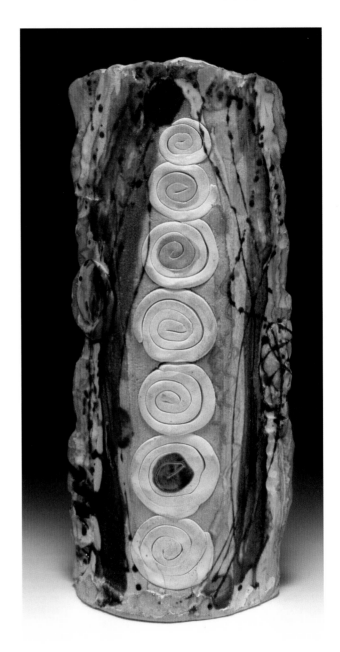

'Standing Form with Spirals', 60 cm high
This page: front; facing page: back view

Working on paintings in acrylics has shown me that in painting you can go on building up layers. This is something which I have brought into ceramics. I am enjoying finding glazes which allow me to go on building layers, by putting a white glaze over a red one, for example, light over dark, so that I can increase the complexity.

The most recent pieces in this series of ceramics are beginning to be semi-figurative, in that as well as having a back and front, they have seven spirals of white clay inserted in the front, which could represent our seven *chakras*, or energy centres.

I am changing my clay: it is becoming more earthy, and this is emphasised by the white glazes trailed on the surface. The glazes seem to 'jump' in the kiln as they volatilise and this has the effect of toasting the clay around the white trailing lines, giving a juicy, buttery fatness to the glazes and a rich colour to the clay.

Standing form,
70 cm high.
Front view

Back view

'Energia', clay painting, 168 cm wide.

Tall forms

The series of seven tall forms was originally inspired
by Rufford Abbey, by the fact that the abbey was
destroyed in the Reformation and that no art had been
produced for that site since. They were successfully
shown there during my 'The Exhilaration of Life' solo
touring show in 2000. The idea came from a small
version made while I was daydreaming. I liked the
form, thought it would look good on a larger scale, and
was commissioned to make a large one by the
collector and patron Lionel Phillips. It is two metres tall,
and looks wonderful with its intense cobalt blues
against the rich greenery of the countryside. More of
these forms are at Broomhill Sculpture Park in Devon.
Outside, they look stunning amongst the green
vegetation: tall, with energy rising upwards from the
earth to the sky, and opening at the top optimistically.
Rich intense inky blues rhythmically waving upwards.

Tall forms at Rufford, 2 m high

Painting

Just as with ceramics, I want my paintings to show immediacy, freshness and spontaneity. My language has bright clear colours, colours which we associate with hot countries and clear light. Colours that vibrate like close harmony singing. I often give my paintings titles which are taken from music, such as *Andante con Brio*. (It is interesting how often composers and jazz musicians talk about music in terms of colour and abstract painting, and I can think of painting in musical terms.) I use big strong colours, some contrasting colours, some quickly trailed lines of colour, some dots, some splashes, swishes, squidges, squiggles, swooshes, marks big and small. All these are like instruments in a jazz band or an orchestra and I use them to create a composition.

  Sometimes my paintings remind me of hugely magnified details of plant or body cells. I like to think I am connected with the rest of the universe through the language of painting and form.

  I am often asked if my large wall and canvas paintings are preparations for the pots, and they are most definitely not. The paintings are paintings. I don't prepare for them either. I do not draw or plan what I am going to do on the canvases or the pots, I just let it happen. It is best if I do not impede the natural flow. In some ways, I feel as if I have no choice. If the natural flow wants me, say, to put a blob of green here, and I resist it, all sorts of problems occur. It sets up a block. It is my subconscious mind which is doing the resisting, by being worried, anxious, unsure, untrusting, and once this starts it will not stop. So that is why I know I have no choice but to trust the natural flow: it knows better than I do.

'Andante con Brio',
acrylic on board.
215 cm high, 245 cm wide

'Purple Swish', watercolour,
61 cm high, 92 cm wide

"Indian Summer", watercolour,
61 cm high, 92 cm wide

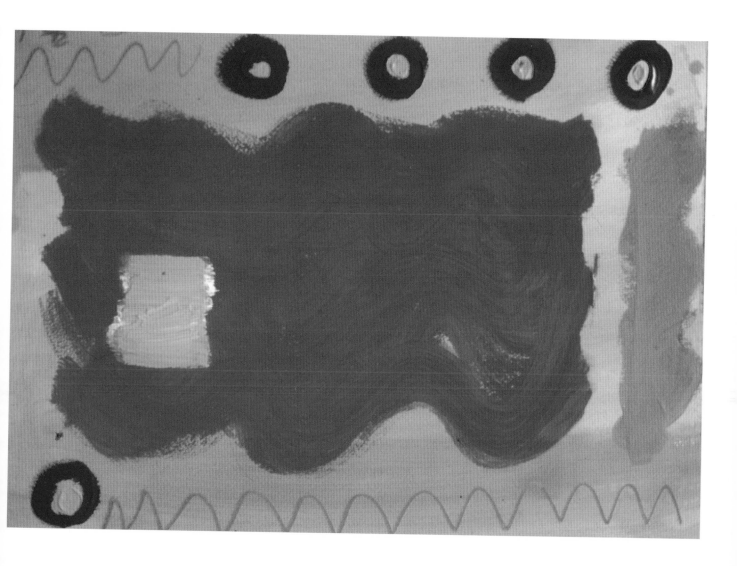

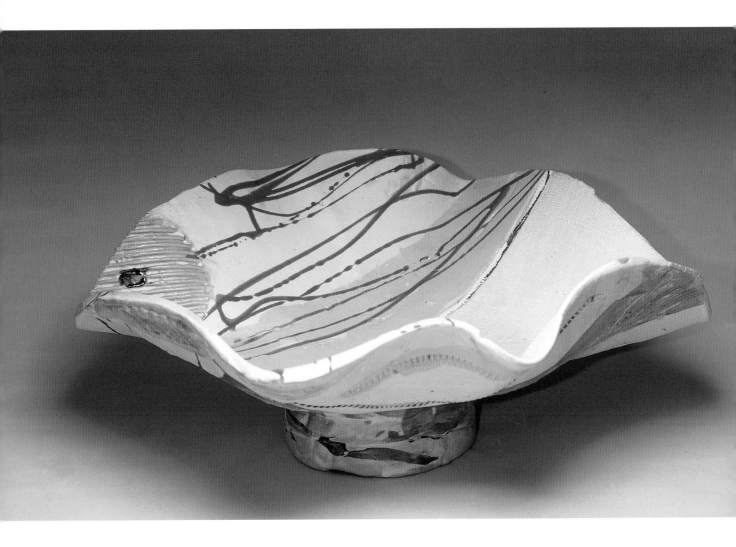

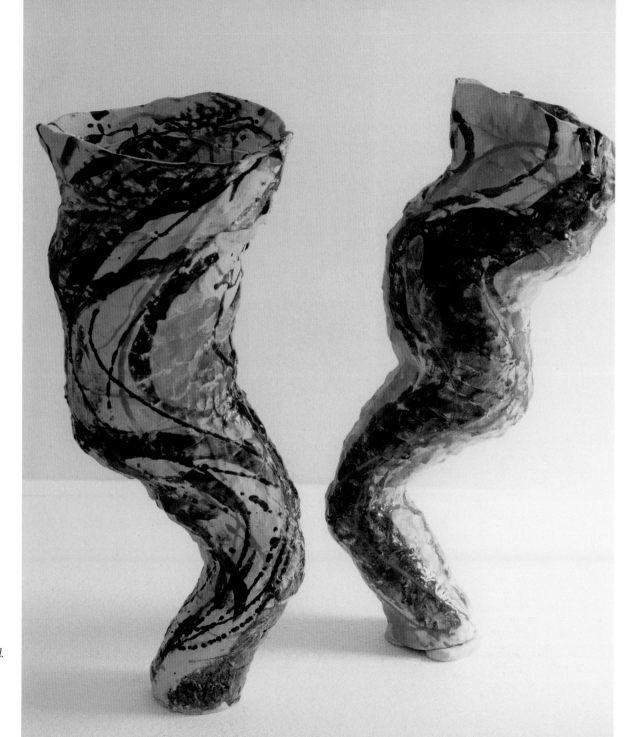

'Dancers', coiled.
122 cm high

'Queen', 30 cm high

*Right: 'Undulating Dish
with a lot of Red',
44 cm wide*

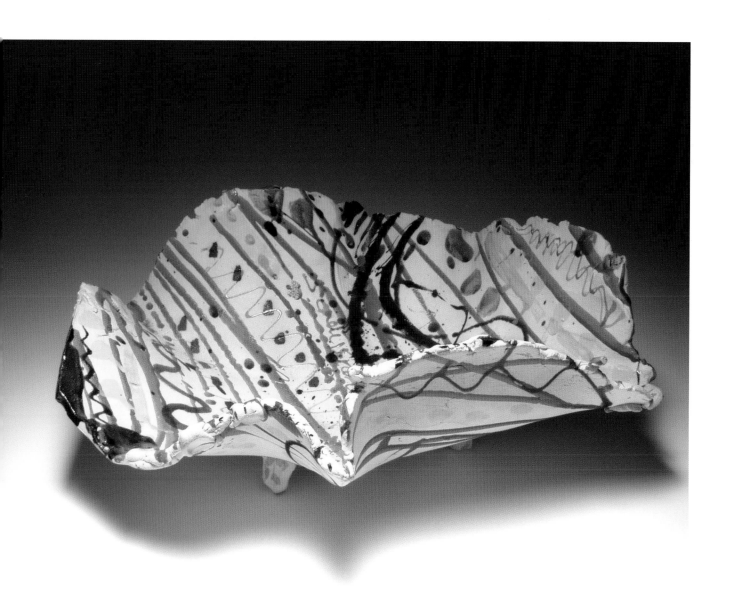

'Woman', 24 cm high

'Charcoal Woman', drawing, 59 cm high, 44 cm wide

Biographical details

1946   Born Tichborne, Hampshire
1969-73 Training at Daisei Pottery, Mashiko, Japan
1973   Crafts Advisory Committee New Craftsman Grant
1985   Residency, University of Texas, USA
1986   South West Arts Project Award
1988   Lecture tour of Australia & New Zealand
       Residency at Gippsland Institute, Australia,
       Residency at Otago Art School, New Zealand
1991   South West Arts Fellowship Award
1992   Lecture tour of South Africa and Namibia
1995   'Sandy Brown: Potter' Westcountry TV programme
       Public commission: 'Tree of Life', Musgrove Hospital, Taunton
2000   Public commission: 'Millennium Map', ceramic, Appledore Arts
       Residency at Rufford Ceramic Centre, Rufford
2001   Lecture tour of India

Coiled bowl, 48 cm wide

'Today it is hard to imagine the European ceramics scene without her. She is famous for her spontaneous, passionate use of clay and colours. Her almost provokingly simple use of form and her strong, energetic brush decorations feed from direct emotion, from confidence in her own intuition and from a portion of childlike anarchy she preserved for herself.

Sandy brown's catalytic, liberating influence on European ceramics in the seventies and above all eighties must not be underestimated. At a time when European ceramics threatened to get stuck between Asian ideals and local traditions, her impetuous, lustful approach to the material demonstrated exciting new possibilities.' Gabi Dewald, *Keramik Magazine*

Technical information

Firing All work is once-fired in either electric or gas kilns to stoneware temperature (1280°C), oxidised.

Bodies For domestic ware and smaller ceramics white St Thomas' clay is used. For larger pieces and life-size figures Craft Crank Mixture is the body. Occasionally red clay is used for softly thrown pieces, and T Material for smaller sculptural work.

Slip Most pots are coated with thick slip or engobe, and for this the following formula is used: ball clay Hyplas 71- 14 parts, china clay - 10 parts, zircon silicate - 3 parts. This slip is also used for slip trailing.

Glazes and colourants A variety of transparent glazes is used, according to the body, and these are brushed on or poured. Colourants are added to make a medium for brushing or trailing the design over the unfired glaze. This design is often in combination with sgraffito made earlier, when the slip is in the appropriate state.
  Cobalt, manganese and copper oxide are used in various proportions for blue, dark brown and green. For yellow, citrus yellow body stain is used, and pink, red, lime and mandarin yellow commercially prepared underglaze colour stains are used in combination with the transparent glaze to produce a wide range of surfaces and colours.

Selected exhibitions

1984 *Two British Potters* - Tokyo
Tableware: New Domestic Pottery - Crafts Council, London, and touring
1985 *British Potters* - Berlin
Summer Show - British Crafts Centre, London
New British Crafts - Dallas, USA
British Ceramics - Pat Barnes Gallery, Chicago
Sandy Brown (Solo show) - Beaux Arts, Bath
1986 *Sandy Brown* (Solo show) - Amalgam, London
Sandy Brown (Solo show) - Aberystwyth Arts Centre, Wales
A Valentines Exhibition - Crafts Council at the Victoria and Albert Museum, London
Inside: Outside - Wita Gardiner Gallery, San Diego, USA
Shape and Decoration - Scottish Gallery, Edinburgh
1987 *British Ceramics* - Munich Museum, Germany
1987-9 *Sandy Brown: The Complete Picture* (Solo show) - Oriel 31, Wales, touring UK
1988 *Sandy Brown* (Solo show) - Meat Market Craft Centre, Melbourne, Australia
Sandy Brown + Takeshi Yasuda - Galerie für Englische Keramik, Marianne Heller, Germany
1989 *The Unique, the Unusual, the Utilitarian* - ProArt Gallery, St Louis, USA

Summer Show - Contemporary Applied Arts, London
Sandy Brown (Solo show) - Visage, Glastonbury
Contemporary Women Artists - Frankfurt
1990 *Contemporary British Ceramics* - Edinburgh College of Art
Sandy Brown: Figuratively Speaking (Solo show) - Oxford Gallery, Oxford
Sandy Brown: New Work - Green Gallery, Tokyo
Free Spirits - Llantarnam Grange Arts Centre, Cwmbran
Sandy Brown + Takeshi Yasuda - Kunst und Keramiek, Holland
1991 *Sandy Brown: Pots & Goddesses* (Solo show) - Plymouth Arts Centre, Plymouth
The Eye of the Beholder - Prema Arts Centre, Dursley
Sandy Brown: Ritual Objects (Solo show) - Contemporary Ceramics, London
Sandy Brown: Tableware (Solo show) - Vincent Gallery, Exeter
Natural Resources - Plymouth City Museum, touring UK and Europe
Beyond the Dovetail - Crafts Council Gallery, London
Colours of the Earth: 20th Century British Ceramics - British Council, touring India & Malaya
The Hall of Dreams - Cleveland Craft Centre, Middlesborough
1992 *Sandy Brown & Takeshi Yasuda* - Galerie für Englische Keramik, Marianne Heller, Germany
Candelabra - ProArt Gallery, St Louis, USA
Sandy Brown: New Work (Solo show) - Alpha House Gallery, Sherborne
International Invitational Exhibition of Ceramic Art - National Museum of History, Taipei, Taiwan
1993 *High Table* - Midland Arts Centre, touring UK
Form and Function - Contemporary Applied Arts, London
Sandy Brown: Sculpture, Ceramics and Painting (Solo show) - Alpha House Gallery, Sherborne
1994 *International Fine Ceramics* - Alpha House Gallery, Sherborne
Ceramics by Sandy Brown and Poh Chap Yeap - Paul Rice Gallery, London
Gifts for Valentines - Crafts Council Shop at the Victoria and Albert Museum, London
With Your Own Face On - Plymouth City Museum, touring UK
Summer Show - Contemporary Applied Arts, London
British Ceramics - Galerie Desko, Brussels, Belgium
Ideal Home: British Art - Galerie Arts and Crafts, Claude André, Brussels, Belgium
1995 *Sandy Brown: New Work* (Solo show) - Alpha House Gallery, Sherborne
Body Language: Figurative Ceramics - Oxford Gallery, Oxford
1996 *Sandy Brown: New Work* - Amalgam, London
Soft Clay - Contemporary Applied Arts, London
A Day with Sandy Brown - Galerie für Englische Keramik, Marianne Heller, Germany
Festival of Ceramics - Aberdeen Art Gallery, Aberdeen, Scotland

1997   *Sandy Brown* (Solo show) - Broomhill Art Hotel, Devon
       Teapots - British Council, touring South America
       Dish of the Day - British Council, touring Europe
       National Festival of Ceramics - Hatfield, Herts
       Gala Opening Exhibition - Contemporary Ceramics, London
       Artists of Fame and Promise - Beaux Arts, Bath
1998   *Earth & Fire Festival* - Rufford Craft Gallery, Rufford
       Frauen in Europe - Marianne Heller Gallery, Heidelberg,
       Germany, and tour
       New European Ceramics - Marianne Heller Gallery, Heidelberg,
       Germany
       Babette's Feast - Galerie für Kunsthandwerk, Munich, Germany
       Cool Clay - 40 CPA Members: Rufford Craft Gallery, Rufford
       Contemporary British Ceramics: Plymouth Arts Centre, Plymouth
1999   *Sandy Brown* (Solo show) - Kunst & Keramik, Deventer, Holland
       Contemporary British Ceramics - Janet Mansfield Gallery,
       Sydney, Australia
       Staatliche Fachschule fur keramik (Solo show) Germany
2000   *The Exhilaration of Life* (Solo show) - Rufford Ceramics Centre &
       Marianne Heller Gallery, Heidelberg, Germany
       A Splash of Colour (Solo show) - Alpha House Gallery, Sherborne
       Steninge International Ceramic Selection 2000 - Steninge Palace,
       Sweden
       British Ceramics 2000 - Grimmerhus Ceramic Museum, Denmark
       Clay at the Crossroads - Winnipeg Art Gallery, Canada
2001   *World Ceramic Exposition* - Korea
       International Ceramics - Kortjik, Belgium
       Painterly Pots - Brewery Arts, Cirencester & Black Swan, Frome
       Sandy Brown (Solo show) - Burton Art Gallery, Bideford
       Sandy Brown in India - Aurodhan Art Gallery, India
2002   *The Golden Age of Ceramics: 50 Years of Pivotal Ceramicists* -
       Red Gallery, Southsea
2003   *Sandy Brown: New Work* - Contemporary Ceramics, London
       Summertime in Heidelberg (Solo show) - Marianne Heller
       Gallery, Heidelberg, Germany
       Steninge World Exhibition of Ceramics - Steninge Palace,
       Sweden, and touring to Norway
       Le Printemps des Potiers - Bandol, France
       International Invitational Cheongju Biennale, Korea

Work in public collections

Victoria & Albert Museum, Aberystwyth Arts Centre, Cleveland Crafts
Centre, Aberdeen Museum & Art Gallery, Eastern Arts Association,
Ulster Museum, Shipley Art Gallery, British Council, Crafts Council of
Great Britain, Bath Contemporary Arts, West Surrey College of Art,
Broomhill Sculpture Park, Pincher Collection, Stoke on Trent City
Museum, Landesgewerbeamt, Baden-Wurtemburg, Karlsruhe,
Germany, World Ceramic Centre, Ichon, Korea, Gippsland Institute,
Australia, Crafts Council of Victoria, Australia, British Embassy, Tokyo,
Dr Hans Thieman, Germany, Winnipeg Museum of Art, Canada

Select bibliography

Birks, Tony, *The Complete Potters Companion,* London 2003
Blandino, Betty, *The Figure in Fired Clay,* London 2002
Dewar, Richard *Stoneware,* London 2002
Flynn, Michael *Human Figure,* London 2002
Genders, Caroline *Sources of Inspiration,* London 2002
Gregory, Ian, *Sculptural Ceramics,* London 1992
Lane, Peter, *Ceramic Form,* London 1998
Ostermann, Matthias, *The Ceramic Surface,* London 2002
Rice, Paul & Christopher Gowing, *British Studio
    Ceramics,* Marlborough 2002
Vincentelli, Moira, *Women in Ceramics,* Manchester 2000
Waal, Edmund de, *Design Sourcebook Ceramics,* London 1999
Waller, Jane, *The Human Form in Clay,* Marlborough 2001
Wood, Karen Ann, *Tableware in Clay,* Marlborough 1999
Zakin, Richard, *Ceramics,* London 1990

Articles in magazines and journals

Arts West: 'Sandy Brown: Leading Questions', June1987
Ceramic Art & Perception (Australia): 'Sandy Brown: The Sculptures',
    No 30, Dec 1997
Ceramics Monthly (USA): 'Sandy Brown and Takeshi Yasuda', May 1992
    'Sandy Brown and Takeshi Yasuda exhibition in Holland' 1991
Ceramic Review No 183, March/April 2000
    'A Potter's Move', No 149 Sept/Oct 1994
    'The Grand Opera of Pots and Food', No 131 Sept 1991
    'A Potters Day', No 124 July/Aug 1990
    'Sandy Brown: Bold, Wild and Dangerous', No 116 March/April 1989
    'Sandy Brown: A Theatre of Colour', No 99 May/June 1986
    'A Potter in Japan', No 96 Nov/Dec 1985
Craft Arts (Australia): 'Recent Ceramics by Sandy Brown', March/June
    1989
    'British Artist in Residence at Gippsland Institute', Sept/Nov 1988
Crafts Magazine: 'Sources of Inspiration', No 152, May/June 1998
    'Sandy Brown and Takeshi Yasuda', April 1988
Keramik Magazin (Germany): 'Die mondebewegte Frau', August/Sept
    2000
    'Sandy Brown and Takeshi Yasuda', No 6, 1992
    'Sandy Brown and Takeshi Yasuda', April 1988
Kerameiki Techni (Greece): 'Sandy Brown: The Exhilaration of Life',
    No 35
Pottery in Australia: 'Colour and Clay', Feb 1989
    'Sandy Brown', Aug 1988
Revue de la Ceramique et du Verre (France): 'Sandy Brown and
    Takeshi Yasuda', No 59 July 1991
    'La Poterie Domestique en Grand Bretagne', No 45 March/April 1989
Studio Pottery (USA): 'Colour and Form', Dec 99